The Discoveries of
ESTEBAN THE BLACK

The Discoveries of
ESTEBAN THE BLACK

Elizabeth Shepherd
ILLUSTRATED WITH PHOTOGRAPHS AND PRINTS

With maps by William Steinel

DODD, MEAD & COMPANY · NEW YORK

TO PETER

THE ILLUSTRATIONS in this book are used through the courtesy of the following sources. Artists and photographers are noted in parentheses.

Bureau of Sport Fisheries and Wildlife, U. S. Department of the Interior: page 16 (Rex G. Schmidt); 17 (Frank M. Blake); 37 (Luther C. Goldman); 42 (Charles L. Cadieux); 59 (Goldman); 68 (Goldman)

The Morocco National Tourist Office, The Kingdom of Morocco: page 5

National Park Service, U. S. Department of the Interior: page 78 (H. Parent); 85

New Mexico State Tourist Bureau: page 75

The New York Public Library, Map Room: page 7

The New York Public Library, Rare Book Division: page 11 (Jacques Le Moyne); 14 (Le Moyne); 25 (Le Moyne); 29 (Gottfried); 33 (Le Moyne); 39 (Le Moyne); 46 (Le Moyne); 72 (George Catlin); 81 (Edward S. Curtis); 89 (Curtis); 93 (Gottfried); 95 (Gottfried); 99 (Curtis); 102 (Curtis); 107 (Curtis)

The Peabody Museum, Harvard University: page 12 (Le Moyne); 23 (Le Moyne); 55 (A. de Batz); 65

Smithsonian Institution National Anthropological Archives, Bureau of the American Ethnology Collection: page 112 (Matilda C. Stevenson)

U. S. Forest Service: page 49 (W. C. Barnes); 51 (Leland J. Prater); 61 (Kenneth W. Parker); 80 (James Buchholz)

The drawing on page 110 is from *The Kachina and the White Man* by Frederick J. Dockstader. Bloomfield Hills, Michigan: The Cranbrook Institute of Science, 1954. Reprinted by permission of the publisher.

Maps by William Steinel

AUTHOR'S NOTE

IN OLD MANUSCRIPTS the black explorer's name is spelled both as Esteban and Estevan. Sometimes the diminutive forms, Estevanico and Estebanillo, appear. Here I have used the preferred modern spelling, Esteban. In the quotations I have preserved the familiar form, Estebanico, or Little Stephen.

In some instances in the quotations I have simplified the sentence structure and punctuation or, within the body of the text, paraphrased words of the explorers. However, the interested reader can easily find the exact words by referring to the sources noted.

For help in working out the routes on the maps I am indebted to the National Park Service and most especially to Ernest W. Kuncl, Supervisory Park Ranger at the Coronado National Monument. William A. Buckley, Jr., Staff Historian for the Florida Board of Parks, was also very helpful.

For the illustrations I would like most particularly to thank the Rare Book Division of The New York Public Library. Most of the prints, drawings, and paintings made in Esteban's century come from volumes in their collection. This is true of the drawings by Jacques Le Moyne de Morgues, the first artist in North America. From his originals, Theodore de Bry made the engravings, first published in 1591. Though most of Le Moyne's sketches were lost, at least one survives: the drawing of the Timucuan chief, which is in The Peabody Museum, Harvard University. The de Bry engraving of the Timucuans preparing for battle and the original painting of various tribes at the Mississippi by the French artist, A. de Batz, dated 1735, also come from The Peabody Museum.

The George Catlin painting comes from The North American Indian Collection of the Rare Book Division. The chart was copied from one thought to have been made by Alonso Alvarez de Pineda during his expedition from Jamaica to Florida and west to Pánuco. The photograph by Matilda C. Stevenson of the kiva interior was taken in 1889.

In the early 1900's, Edward S. Curtis photographed many North American Indian tribes, some still living much as they did in Esteban's time. Many native North American plants and animals encountered by Esteban can still be found in some places along his trail, and photographs of some of these have been included.

—E. S.

CONTENTS

CAST OF SPANISH NOTABLES MENTIONED IN THE TEXT

Pánfilo de Narváez, former governor of Cuba and commander of the expedition of 1528

Álvar Núñez Cabeza de Vaca, treasurer and provost marshall of the Narváez expedition

Alonso del Castillo Maldonado, a captain with the Narváez expedition

Andrés Dorantes, a captain with the Narvaez expedition and master of Esteban

Antonio de Mendoza, first Viceroy of New Spain (Mexico)

Friar Marcos de Niza, Father Provincial of the Franciscan Order in New Spain

LIST OF MAPS

CHRONOLOGY

October 14, 1492   Christopher Columbus discovers San Salvador

1496   Santo Domingo settled by Spaniards. First European settlement in the New World.

1511   Cuba settled by Diego de Velázquez

1513   Juan Ponce de León begins exploration of Florida

1513   Vasco Nuñez de Balboa discovers the Pacific Ocean

1519   Alonso Alvarez de Pineda explores Gulf Coast from Florida to Tampico, searching for passage to the Pacific

1519-21   Hernán Cortés conquers the Aztecs of Mexico

1528   Pánfilo de Narváez lands on the west coast of Florida

September, 1534   Survivors of Narváez expedition start inland across Texas. Discover New Mexico and Arizona.

July 24, 1536   Four survivors reach Mexico City

March 7, 1538   Esteban starts north from Culiacán

April 27, 1538   Esteban discovers ancient Zuni pueblo of Hawikuh

1539-43   Hernando de Soto explores southeastern region of North America

1540-42   Francisco Vásquez de Coronado explores southwestern region of North America

PROLOGUE

The Trial

It was hot, and the tall bearded man had been walking all day. He walked slowly now, but he did not stop. On the flat tableland there were no trees to offer shade.

Ahead of him the gray walls of the town shimmered in the heat. Behind him came hundreds of men, women, and children. They had followed him here all the way from their homes in the valley far to the south. They were people whom white explorers called Indians.

In the town lived other Indians. Now these people stopped working in the fields and around their homes. They stood on the flat roofs of their houses and watched the crowd coming across the treeless land. They did not know these people from the south. What did their coming mean?

When the tall man had almost reached the town, or pueblo, the elders dropped ladders over the wall and climbed down.

They stared at the leader. He looked like no one they had ever seen.

He was black. His skin was as black as soot from a campfire, and his lips were swollen as though from eating chili peppers. His beard was thick and curly.

The town elders wondered at his strange appearance. Still, they invited him into the pueblo with a few of his followers. The others built campfires below the wall. There they waited for their leader.

The black man told the elders a strange story. He was called Esteban el Negro, or Stephen the Black. He knew the secrets of the Earth Mother and the Sky Father. He had crossed a great ocean and climbed many mountains. He had come from the land beyond the sunrise.

Hundreds and hundreds of white men were coming after him, the black man said. They wanted gold and emeralds. If the pueblo people gave them these things, the white men would go their way in peace. If not, the white men would take everything. They had sticks that shot lightning and made thunder.

The elders could not believe this story. Could there truly be people as pale as wind clouds or sticks that made thunder? The elders frowned. No one in all that land had ever seen such people. This strange black-skinned man must be a spy from an enemy tribe. Perhaps he was some kind of sorcerer. Certainly there was something dangerous about him. The elders did not want him in their pueblo.

They led the black man to a square house just beyond the pueblo wall. Its door, like the doors of the houses within the pueblo itself, opened from the roof. Esteban went down the ladder and the town elders pulled it up behind him. He was their prisoner. When they found out who he was and why he had come with all those strangers, then they would know what to do with him.

All this happened more than four hundred years ago. And no one has yet learned Esteban's whole story. Probably no one ever will. But from legends told by Indians and from reports written by white men who knew him, historians and geographers and anthropologists know much about his adventures in North America. Here is the story the pueblo people were trying to learn.

1

The Beginning

"And now that I have given an account of the ships, it may be well to record also who those are and where from whom it pleased God to rescue from all these dangers and hardships. . . . The fourth man was Estebánico, an Arab Negro from Azemmour."

WITH these words Esteban's name became part of American history. And these words tell all that is known of his early life.

Azemmour is a city on the northwest coast of Africa. It stands at the mouth of a large slow-moving river, which makes a good harbor. In 1513 the Portuguese captured Azemmour. They held it all during Esteban's life.

As a small boy, Esteban could see the Portuguese warships

From the ship that carried him into slavery, Esteban saw Azemmour for the last time. The city today looks much as it did then.

anchored in the harbor. Beyond the ships, waves rolled in from the Atlantic Ocean. The waves made a long foaming line as they broke against the reddish waters of the river.

But often the warships headed out, across the breaking waves, into the ocean. They attacked Spanish ships carrying gold from the Americas. They protected their own ships carrying slaves north to Spanish markets, for the Spaniards paid well for slaves. They needed them to work in their new colonies across the Atlantic.

The Portuguese made Esteban a slave. He was probably

taken to Spain as soon as he was able to do a man's work, at the age of ten or twelve. He lived in Spain, for a short time at least, because his Spanish master, Andrés Dorantes, said that Esteban was a Christian. Spanish rulers in those days insisted that everyone living in their country become a Catholic.

In June of 1527, Esteban sailed with his master to the New World. They were among six hundred others, mostly soldiers and future settlers, all crammed into the five ships commanded by the conquistador Pánfilo de Narváez.

The ships landed first at Hispaniola, where Christopher Columbus had started the first Spanish colony in the New World. Then they stopped in Cuba to get supplies and to make repairs. Unlike many other slaves, Esteban was not taken off to work in the plantations of either colony. He was needed to carry supplies into the wilderness that was North America. His master was one of Narváez's captains, and they were sailing on to explore the mainland.

Narváez had the commission from the King of Spain to explore, conquer, and settle all the unknown land from the Florida peninsula to the Rio Grande. (No Spaniard could start on an expedition without such a commission.) Eight years earlier, Alonso de Pineda, an explorer looking for a way to the Pacific, had made a rough chart of the coast. But no European, or African either, knew what lay beyond the coast. The chart-maker had heard rumors of seven great cities to the north. Hernán Cortés had heard the same stories when he conquered Mexico City. With each retelling the cities be-

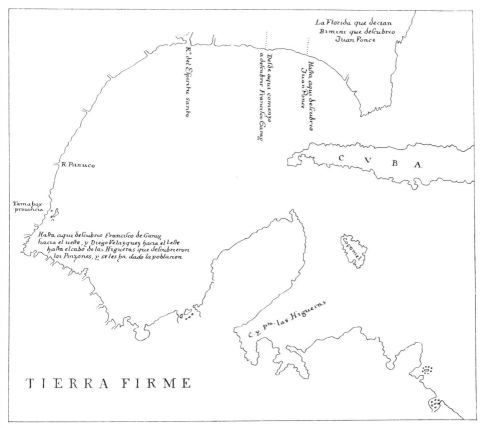

With just such a chart, Pánfilo de Narváez left Cuba on February 21, 1528. This one is thought to have been made by Alonso de Pineda, an explorer searching for a passage to the Pacific Ocean.

came richer and grander. It was said that even the streets shone with emeralds, and the rivers ran over golden sands.

Such stories passed away the long sea voyage. And for Esteban and the other slaves they gave hope of freedom. In those days, the Spaniards often paid their slaves for doing extra work. And when the slaves had enough money to pay back their purchase price, they were freed. The Spanish officers would pay well for such work if the expedition found gold. In the gleaming cities of North America, Esteban might quickly earn his freedom.

With some such thoughts, perhaps, Esteban saw the western shore of Florida appear out of the afternoon haze. That was on April 12, 1528. From then on, his life story is part of our history.

2

A Golden Rattle

"On Good Friday, Governor Narváez landed with as many men as his little boats would hold. And when we arrived at the huts we had seen, we found them abandoned. The Indians had fled that night in their canoes. One house was so large that it could hold more than 300 people. The others were smaller. We found a gold rattle among their nets."

These words were written by Cabeza de Vaca, the treasurer of the expedition, when he made his report of the landing in North America. Though he wrote it ten years later, two things still stood out in his memory: the big house and the golden toy.

The golden toy! To Pánfilo de Narváez, and to the soldiers and settlers who landed with him, the toy proved the old

9

stories were true. Somewhere in this land, beyond the dunes, beyond the bay, there were truly cities of gold. How rich their people must be if they left gold toys lying about!

Esteban wriggled his bare toes in the hot, dry sand. He saw huts made of sticks and palm leaves. The big house was like the others except for its size. In Africa, the Berbers made the same sort of huts. They were poor people, Esteban knew, and their babies had no gold toys.

The builders of these huts must be poor too. If so, where had the golden rattle come from? Perhaps the hut builders were slaves. Perhaps they worked in the Seven Cities of Gold.

Narváez seemed to think so. Without waiting for the Indian inhabitants to come back, he called his people together and declared himself Governor.

"This village and all the land around it belongs to the King of Spain," he said. "It shall be called La Bahia de la Cruz." Then the new Governor of the Bay of the Cross received Esteban's master and the other officers. The bay was now Spanish territory.

And on Easter Sunday, when the Indians finally did come back, the new Governor ignored them. He ignored their angry shouts. He pretended not to see their shaking fists. And at last, still shouting, the Indians paddled away again in their canoes. They were Timucuan Indians, we now know.

Three days later, the Spanish soldiers captured four Indians and brought them before Narváez. Again the Spaniard turned his back. But this time he commanded someone to

Landing on the Florida coast about thirty-six years after Narváez, a French artist drew the Timucuans he met, as well as their houses and surrounding trees. Like the Timucuans Esteban saw, they hunted wild turkeys and deer, and planted corn.

question the Indians for him. By doing this he hoped they would understand that he was a great and important man, too great and too important to talk with them.

Though Cabeza did not say so in his report, it seems likely that Esteban was the interpreter. He did all the talking with

Even a Timucuan chief wore little but tattoos, each recording an important battle or hunt. Pricked into the skin with a sharp fishbone, the design was rubbed with soot.

the Indians at later times. He spoke Spanish easily. And though he did not know the language of the four captives, he had the golden rattle to help show what Narváez wanted.

"Gold?" he asked. "Do you have gold?" He pointed to the rattle and, with his hands, shaped huge piles of gold, castles of gold.

The Indians answered with signs and words. To the north,

they told him, there was everything the strangers wanted. There was a large town called Apalachen. Its people were very rich. They were the richest of all the peoples in that region.

Esteban watched the Indians closely. He was trying to learn each sign they made, each word they spoke. But he was puzzled. To the north he could see nothing but scrub oaks and pine trees growing low and twisted over the flat sandy land.

"How far is this Apalachen?" he asked.

"Very far," the Indians replied. "It is many days journey from here."

Then one of the Spaniards stepped forward impatiently. He gave the black interpreter a handful of corn. Like many others with Narváez, he had come to settle in the new land. He was looking for a place to build a home and plant fields.

Esteban showed the corn to the Indians. The people of Mexico grew corn, he had heard. Perhaps these people did too. He knew the expedition needed fresh food. The voyage from Cuba had taken far longer than any one planned. Supplies of food were low and getting lower. One ship had gone back to Cuba for more food. But it might not return for many weeks. Until it did, Narváez's people had to find things to eat.

The Indians looked at the dried kernels in Esteban's hand. They spoke softly together. Then they led him to a small field at the far end of the bay. There, corn was growing.

Some coastal Indians stored corn and melons along the riverbanks in solid houses of stone and earth.

The soldiers ran from row to row. They stripped the ripe ears from the stalks, and then the green ones. Before the sun set that day, the corn was gone.

But Esteban had a new key to freedom. He could talk with the Indians. They understood his signs. He understood theirs. The corn was the proof. Unfortunately they had no more corn, and they grew no other crops.

3

The March into the Wilderness

". . . they left there in search of yonder province called Apalachen. They took with them as guides the Indians whom they had captured; . . . to reach Apalachen—that was the thing in the world they most wanted, as much because of the long road as because of their great need for provisions."

On May 2, Narváez and three hundred of his strongest men set off for Apalachen with the captured Indians as guides. The four remaining ships sailed ahead with the women and the men who were too weak to march or fight. They would wait for Narváez in the harbor called Espíritu Santo that was marked on the old chart. There the three hundred "strongest" men would join them when they had conquered Apalachen. At least, that was Narváez's plan.

15

The guides led the Spanish explorers through pine forests and cypress swamps like this, with Spanish moss hanging from the trees.

Few of the three hundred were in good condition for a march into an unknown country. Except for the men who had joined the expedition in Cuba, all had been living on ships for almost a year. None but the slaves had done much physical work.

Besides, Narváez had given them little food, and most of that was rotten. Now, setting off, each man had two pounds of sea biscuit and a bit of salt pork—nothing more. There was no other food left.

Some days the marchers found corn in the villages they passed. They ate the corn, and they must have eaten what berries they found. For some reason no one hunted rabbits or deer, though these animals were everywhere.

From time to time the men saw Indians lurking behind the trees. Twice the soldiers were able to capture a few men so that Esteban could ask about Apalachen.

Always the captives agreed with the guides. The Apalachees were the most fierce and warlike people of the region. They had many villages, but Apalachen was the largest and richest of all.

As the hot spring turned into a hotter summer, the marchers plodded on. Mostly they followed the shore. Yet without guides they would soon have lost the trail. In that region the Indians always walked single file, damaging the underbrush as little as possible. This kept their enemies from guessing how many they were. But for the Spaniards it made a difficult trail to follow. And it meant that the officers, and even Narváez himself, must often go on foot like the common

The Spaniards were so impressed by the mother opossum's care of her young that no one lifted a crossbow to kill these animals.

Apalachen

Choctawhatchee Bay

Six men die
of thirst

Man lost
by drowning

One slave
ambushed
and killed

Apalachicola River

Ochlockonee River

Bay of Horses

September 22, 1528
Five boats launched

Four ships sail
for Espíritu Santo

About one year later,
ships return to Cuba

GULF OF MEXICO

1528
LA FLORIDA

Scale in miles

0   20   40

ATLANTIC OCEAN

Find corn in Indian village. Ambushed again

June 17
Meet Indian in painted deerskin riding on back of another Indian

May 16
Ambushed by two hundred Indians. Take six Indians as hostages. Find corn. Explore river to sea.

April 15
Narváez takes possession of first Indian village

April 13, 1528
Narváez enters bay

Tampa Bay

One ship returns to Cuba for supplies

soldiers and slaves. But then the horses that had lived through the voyage were too weak to be ridden much anyway.

At last, after six weeks of marching along these trails, of wading through swamps, of swimming across rivers, Narváez and his men came to a small lake.

"Apalachen!" Their guides whispered the name fearfully.

On the opposite shore stood a village. It was larger than other villages they had seen. But was this truly the golden city they had come so far to conquer?

There was no one to ask. The guides had disappeared into the wilderness.

4

The First City of Gold

"We gave many thanks to God for being so near it . . .
Now our sufferings could come to an end after the long
and weary march over bad trails. . . . At last we found ourselves where we wished to be and where we had been told
so much food and gold would be had. That made us forget
a great deal of our hardships and weariness."

CABEZA de Vaca led an advance guard forward. They saw
a few women and children moving about in the village. But
where were the men? Were they planning an ambush?

A few soldiers pushed into the first house while the others
held their crossbows ready. They found no one inside. They
ran their swords through a woven basket in one corner. Still,
no one appeared.

21

Slowly the soldiers went from house to house. They searched the whole village and then the huts scattered in the forest nearby. Not one man did they find.

The soldiers laid down their weapons and began to look for hidden treasures. In this Governor Narváez and the others soon joined them. They dragged out deerskins and baskets from the houses. They ripped leaves from the roofs. They poked over the ashes of cold campfires.

They found not so much as a golden rattle. Either the Apalachees had no gold or they had hidden it in some other place.

Still, the soldiers did find another sort of gold. In the houses, ears of golden corn hung drying under the roofs. Husked kernels were piled high in baskets. Soon the soldiers had the women grinding the dried corn for mush.

Esteban watched the women. They seemed all bones under their cotton shawls. The children wore nothing at all. Their naked bodies were dirty and their long black hair was tangled and dull. These people were not rich, Esteban knew.

A horse shrieked. Esteban turned quickly. The animal had fallen. An arrow was buried so deep in its side that only the feathers showed.

From fallen trees and bushes, Apalachees jumped up. Shaking off the leaves that had hidden them, they raised their bows. The Spaniards ran for cover as arrows rained about them.

Then, just as suddenly as they had appeared, the Indians

The warlike Apalachees organized for battle with a formal ceremony. Once feared far and wide by neighboring tribes, their name survives in the word Appalachian and in place names throughout their former territory.

ran off, a custom Esteban soon learned about. It meant they had used up all their arrows. The Indians had to make new arrows or gather up the old ones before they could attack again.

A few hours later the Apalachees came back, peacefully this time, to ask for their women and children. Narváez consented, but he took the chief for a hostage instead. This was a mistake, for the Indians would never attack if their wives and children were in danger. Now they would fight in earnest to rescue their chief.

The first raid came before dawn the next morning. On the following day, about two hundred Apalachees from another village joined in a second raid. That day and almost every day thereafter, the Apalachees attacked. They wounded many Spaniards and some horses too.

"The good armor we wore was no help," Cabeza de Vaca wrote later. And of course the slaves and many Spaniards too wore no armor at all.

"There were some people," Cabeza continued, "who swore that they had seen two red oak trees, each as thick as the lower part of a man's leg, pierced through by arrows."

Against these skillful archers, the proud Spanish soldiers proved no match. By the time they had aimed their guns or crossbows, the enemy had vanished in the underbrush. Narváez could not conquer the Apalachee Indians.

And as he saw his men dying from arrow wounds, from disease, and from starvation, he knew that the Apalachees would soon conquer them.

Their only hope was to escape. Yet scouts had explored the country in all directions. It was full of swamps and thick forests, they discovered, just as the Apalachee chief had told Esteban.

But beyond the swamps to the south lay a shallow bay, the

Tipping their arrows with burning moss, the Apalachees attacked swiftly. As their enemies ran from the burning huts, the Apalachees disappeared into the forest.

chief had said, and that bay gave into the sea. From the shores of that bay Narváez and his soldiers might signal the ships and be rescued.

So Narváez gave marching orders, and after eight or nine desperate days of slogging through swamps, dodging Indian arrows the whole way, they reached the bay.

There once again their hopes were dashed. To reach the open sea they would have to walk along the shore for many days, or so it appeared. But many men were ill with dysentery or malaria. Few were strong enough to try such a march.

"We have just one chance left," Cabeza de Vaca declared. "We'll build boats ourselves and sail out of the bay."

"Boats!" Narváez sneered. "Do you know how to build a boat? And what would we build it with? We have no tools, no rigging, nothing."

Esteban looked from one officer to the other. Their situation seemed hopeless.

5

La Bahia de los Caballos

". . . The next day God provided that one man should come, saying that he would make some pipes out of wood. With a bag of deerskin, the pipes might be made into bellows. We were in such a state that we were ready to accept anything that sounded helpful. We told him to go to work."

LIKE many of the others, Governor Narváez was suffering from malaria. Apparently he was too sick to see what this man's idea meant. He let Cabeza de Vaca give the order. The bellows were made.

In and out, in and out Esteban pumped the deerskin bag, forcing the air out in long spurts. The fire flared up. Slaves piled on wood and more wood. Hotter and hotter the fire burned.

Esteban handed the bellows to the next man. Wading into the cove, he splashed water over his face and arms. The water cooled his sunburned shoulders and helped the itching of the insect bites. The mosquitoes had missed no part of his body, it seemed.

Then Esteban returned to the fire and again took his turn at the bellows. He watched the soldiers bringing their cross-bows and swords and lances. One by one they came with their weapons, which had proved so useless against the Apa-lachees. Melted down and pounded into axes and hammers and saws, these weapons might help the men escape.

In a few days, tools were ready and work on five boats had started. Two carpenters, one a Greek and one a Portuguese, gave directions.

The soldiers rode off to raid the fields of a village nearby. Their horses scared the villagers, who had never seen any such animals before, and so the soldiers were able to get corn and squash and beans.

Other men tried fishing in the river. The Apalachees soon stopped that. They killed ten men, their arrows going right through the Spanish armor.

After this, the Spaniards used their horses for meat. That was why they named the cove "La Bahia de los Caballos" (The Bay of the Horses). Many years later the explorers with Hernando de Soto found the bones of the horses and the re-mains of the fires.

Sometime that summer, Narváez's own ships saw the smoke

*Always ready to share their corn supplies with strangers, the coastal
Indians were often cruelly repaid for their generosity.*

from those fires. Thinking it came from Apalachee campfires, the ships sailed on past. They searched the coast for
almost a year. They never found their commander and his
men. They finally returned to Cuba and reported the expedition lost.

Meanwhile, Narváez's men finished their small boats and
launched them in the shallow bay. Each boat was about 22
elbows long (or 22 arm lengths, measuring from fingertip
to elbow). Each had a mast, oars, and a rudder of oak.

Course of the Five Small Boats

Scale in miles

0   20   40

Sabine River

Sabine Lake

Mississippi River

Hurricane

See Indian
smoke signals

GULF of

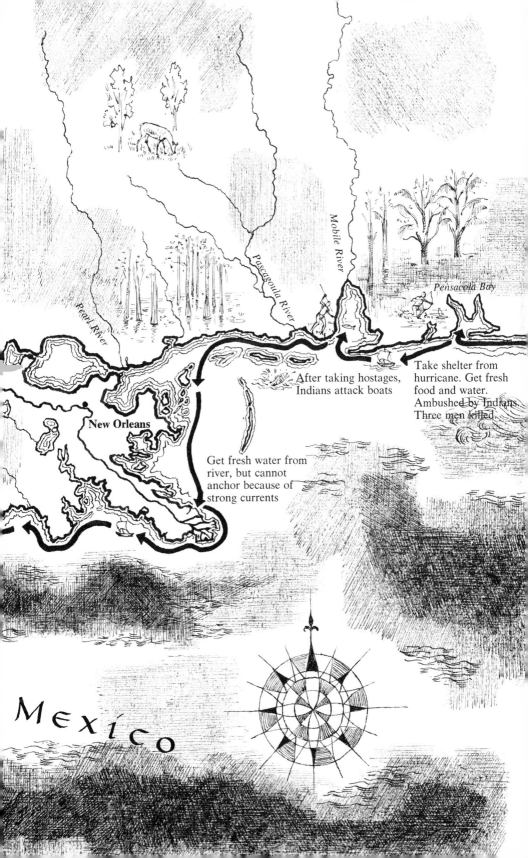

Mobile River

Pascagoula River

Pearl River

Pensacola Bay

After taking hostages,
Indians attack boats

Take shelter from
hurricane. Get fresh
food and water.
Ambushed by Indians.
Three men killed

New Orleans

Get fresh water from
river, but cannot
anchor because of
strong currents

M e x i c o

On the first day of autumn the men loaded the boats with their supplies of corn and what little extra clothing they had. Even then the boats did not sink, and they did not leak. The men cheered. Their work had succeeded. By stuffing palmetto husks between the planks and then smearing pine resin over the outside, they had made the five hulls water-tight.

Water did splash in over the sides when the crews of each boat climbed on board. With 45 to 50 men to a crew, the sides were barely a hand's breadth above water.

Esteban belonged to the crew commanded by two cap-tains, his master Andrés Dorantes and Alonso del Castillo. Like other slaves, Esteban sat at the oars. But though they pulled at their oars with both hands, the boat hardly moved, it was so heavy.

"Raise sail," Dorantes commanded. Crewmen yanked ropes —palmetto husks braided together with hairs from the horses' manes and tails. Up went the sails—patchworks of shirts and capes and breeches sewn together.

The sails filled, the boat tipped to one side, and water poured in. The new sailors bailed furiously, using hands, helmets, anything to get the water out.

Dorantes shoved the tiller over. As the boat turned, it steadied itself. Once again the men cheered. The boat would sail without danger of capsizing. Later, the men raised the sides by adding wood. This made the boats a little easier to control.

On one island near shore, Esteban found a good supply of smoked meat and fish. Here, one Indian brings an alligator to the drying rack, while another fans the fire.

All the helmsmen turned their boats. Though no one knew how to lay a course, that hardly mattered. They had to go with the wind. The captains had but one choice of direction.

Day after day the wind came from the northeast, driving the boats steadily westward. Even if they missed the harbor, if the wind held they might reach Mexico and perhaps even Pánuco, the port that the Spanish conqueror Cortés had settled on the Rio Pánuco. For all his grumbling, Narváez himself could not ask for a better course.

They kept within sight of land and when the wind was light, Esteban and other slaves were sent ashore to look for fresh water and food. Though Esteban did not know how to swim, he did not need to. The water was seldom deeper than his waist.

Sometimes he found the eggs of shore birds or strings of fish that the Indians had left hanging on racks to dry. Sometimes he found nothing. Then the crew ate corn that they had dried for the voyage.

The main problem was drinking water. They had brought along horsehide bottles filled with fresh water. But the hides had rotted and spoiled the water. Now the men had nothing to drink except water they found along the marshy shores.

Once, Esteban met Indians who gave him good water. In another bay Indians took the Greek carpenter and an African slave ashore for water. Unfortunately these Indians mistook the strangers for slave hunters from the Spanish colony in Hispaniola. Often the colonists did raid the coast and carry off Indian slaves. So now the Indians attacked, wounding many of Narváez's men and killing several others. In 1541, De Soto's men found the carpenter's dagger, but no trace of the African.

After this, the five boats stayed farther off shore. Then one night the outside edge of a hurricane swept them out of sight of land. Blinded by wind and rain, the crews soon lost touch with one another. One morning just before dawn, Esteban's voyage was over. His boat was driven onto a sandy shore. The day was November 5, or so Dorantes reckoned. They did not know what had happened to the other four boats and their crews.

6

Shipwrecked

"Finding themselves near the shore, they began to move on hands and feet, crawling to land into some hollows. . . . Half an hour later 100 Indian archers joined them. Our fright was such that, whether tall or little, it made them look like giants to us. We could not hope to defend ourselves as there were scarcely three of us who could stand on their feet."

Esteban got up slowly, brushing the sand off his chest and belly. He was a tall man, but the Indians were even taller than he, their skin the color of wet pine bark.

Esteban spoke first, trying his few Indian words. The Indians looked at him blankly. Then one man spoke. His language was different from any Esteban had heard. But from

35

the Indian's signs Esteban understood they were sad to see
people in such poor condition. They had several men building fires behind the dunes so that the strangers could warm
themselves until the Indian women could come with food.

Shivering with worry as much as cold, Esteban spent the
night. If these Indians wished to kill them all, this time there
was no escape.

The Indians returned in the morning, bringing fish and
sweet roots. The men carried bows but made no move to use
them. Silently, they watched the shipwrecked men eat.

By signs Esteban learned that their boat had been wrecked
on a long narrow island of sand and marsh. The Indians of
that island were Karankawans. It was their custom to greet
visitors—be they friends or strangers or, even, enemies—with
gifts. Because they valued food more than anything, they gave
food. They also gave bows and arrows as tokens of their
friendship, and these offered also a means of getting food.

When the shipwrecked men were strong enough to walk,
the Karankawans led them to their camp. Since these people
planted no crops, they had no one village. They camped
wherever the food was, and moved on when it was gone.
Sometimes they hunted small game, such as birds and rabbits.
Mostly they fished or gathered oysters in the bays and rivers
of that region.

The women dug roots, picked berries, and gathered other
plants. When they had nothing else to do, they wove rushes
and reeds into mats for their houses. By tying these mats to a

As Esteban came ashore, hundreds of whooping cranes rose awkwardly into the air. Few of these great white birds survive today.

frame of poles, the women built a small house. Each time the band moved, each woman took her mats with her. In the new camp she set up her house again.

By adding a few mats to their houses the women had space for the strangers. Each family took in one or two men. They gave their deerskins to the sickest of the Spaniards.

Esteban could feel wind through the straw walls and the damp creeping through the floor mat. Still, it was good to be on land again after the long days in the boat.

The boat commanded by Cabeza de Vaca had also been wrecked on the island, Esteban soon learned. Cabeza and his fellow survivors were camped with another band of Karakawans about an hour's distance off to the west. When the men were strong enough to walk, the two groups met.

"There is not much we can do about our boats," Cabeza said. "But things could be worse. If our ships sail past, we shall surely see them."

The others agreed.

Meanwhile four men volunteered to try to reach Pánuco for help. A Karankawan who knew the shore trail well offered to guide them.

For those on the island, however, hope of rescue soon faded. Many of the Spaniards were sick and many died. Worse still, the Karankawans caught their diseases, in particular, dysentery. They too began dying.

Day and night their shamans, or medicine men, worked trying to drive out the evil spirits which, they believed, had caused the illness. Finally, the shamans declared that it was the visitors who were the evil spirits. They should be driven out of the camp and killed.

One old man had another idea. "Let the visitors cure the sick," he said. "If they fail, then let them starve."

Captain Castillo had watched the shamans with special interest, perhaps because his own father was a doctor. More likely the captain was interested in the food with which the shamans were paid. Whatever his interest, the Karankawans chose him as their new doctor. (In the other camp, Cabeza de Vaca was forced to become a doctor too.)

Carefully Castillo examined his first patient. The whole

Lying on benches made for their cures, one patient inhales smoke from burning seeds. A medicine man blows on the other's forehead.

camp was watching. Esteban had seen the shamans make small cuts in the patient's skin. Through these cuts, they sucked out the evil which they thought caused the pain. Castillo did not try that. Instead, Esteban heard the Spaniard blessing the patient. Then Castillo blew on the painful area. He prayed and made the sign of the cross over the man.

To Esteban's surprise the patient got up and declared himself cured. His family rushed to give the new "medicine man" food. They offered him a wife, for such a powerful "medicine man" could support a wife well.

Castillo treated patient after patient. And all recovered.

Perhaps by now the disease had run its course. The patients brought food to the strangers again. To do this they themselves often had to go without eating.

That winter there were few fish. The women dug roots when they could, but often the bay was too choppy or too cold. Esteban tried to help the men stake out their fish traps. When they laughed at his efforts, he dug roots with the women instead. The women teased him when they first saw him wriggling his long hoe in the mud. But they needed his help. And he soon gained skill in pulling out the roots from the muck. He had to learn how to get food for himself. That was the only way to survive.

And surely Esteban was thinking about his future survival as well. If the settlers in Pánuco sent a rescue ship, what should he do? In Pánuco he would be doomed to a life of slavery in the mines, for his master would certainly sell him to pay for his own trip back to Spain. Here, Esteban was a slave to his own hunger, but he was as free as any man.

By February the roots began to sprout. This made them too bitter to eat. Then the Karankawans and their uninvited guests waded across the bay to the mainland. For the next two months they camped along that shore and ate oysters.

About the first of April the Karankawans returned to the island for blackberries. Now all the Indians of the island celebrated the coming of spring. Soon the fish would run again. The Karankawans sang and danced. With heavy feet Esteban joined the happy Indians.

7

Flight into Slavery

". . . and there were these few Christians who had escaped from the hunger and cold of the winter. . . . The Indians took them across another inlet for certain things which they gave them."

ONLY nineteen Christians had survived the winter. (By calling them Christians, the historian, who recorded those lines, avoided any confusion with the heathen Indians.) Of these nineteen survivors three men, including Cabeza de Vaca, were very ill. Among those well enough to leave the island for Pánuco were Esteban, Dorantes, and Castillo.

Esteban was sent on ahead. If he stumbled into a bog or aroused a fierce animal, his cries would warn the others.

But he did not stumble or startle any wild animals. He

41

Walking along the shore at night, Esteban sometimes heard the deep, low growl of a bobcat.

found a good trail which led westward. For three days and nights the group followed this trail, resting only when they could walk no longer. When they saw kelp or other seaweed along the shore, they ate that. Sometimes they caught a few of the sand crabs that scampered about the beach. Mostly they chewed on the tough beach grass and kept going. They felt certain the Karankawans would pursue them.

Late on the fourth day, Esteban realized he had taken a poor turning. A wide stretch of water lay in front of them, and soon the trail ended.

But off in the distance Esteban could see sand dunes, slowly darkening and turning purple as the sun disappeared. Dunes!

"It's the harbor," he cried. "The harbor!" An inlet leading

to a wide protected bay, high dunes in the distance—this seemed to match Pineda's description perfectly. It must be Espíritu Santo, the harbor Narváez had sent the ships to find. But there were no ships there. Still, the men felt better. They were back on the map of the known world. And once they got across the inlet they would not have far to walk. The remaining distance to Pánuco was, they believed, no greater than the distance they had already walked.

Of course, the trail they picked up was longer and far more difficult than they expected. Before they had gone far, they were prisoners of another band of Karankawans. The Indians divided up the strangers, keeping Esteban, Dorantes, and Castillo at the shore to pick blackberries. Later that summer Esteban learned that the other Spaniards had been killed somewhere down the coast.

Esteban's new masters fished and hunted in the marshes all summer long, moving their camp every two or three days. He and his fellow prisoners dragged the dugout canoes over sand bars and pushed them through the shallow muddy places. They did woman's work: digging roots, tying mats for houses, carrying mats when the band moved. And endlessly, it seemed, they carried heavy loads of drinking water. For since they were surrounded by salt marshes, there was little water there that was fit to drink.

As if the heavy work in the hot sun were not torture enough, the Indians delighted in tormenting their four captives. Arrow in hand, a Karankawan might spring upon Este-

— Píneda Map
Modern Map

R. del Espíritu Santo

R. Pánuco

C V B A

Youths throw balls, shoot arrows at targets, and race to see who gets winded first. Such training made them skillful hunters.

ban. The black man went on adding twigs to his bundle. He had to gather enough to keep the fire going all night. That was the only way to ward off mosquitoes. If he failed, he would be beaten.

"Coward, I'm going to kill you," the Karankawan seemed to be saying. The dialect he spoke was not like the one spoken back on the island.

Esteban tried to ignore the awful voice. Did the Karankawan mean what he said this time?

A sharp jab in his chest made Esteban grip the bunch of twigs tightly. Then he heard the Indian howling with laughter.

The little boys were as bad as their elders. They threw stones and clods of earth at the prisoners. They laughed if the men so much as winced.

But for that matter these people tested themselves as much as their slaves. A Karankawan would die rather than suffer an insult. At the slightest excuse they attacked their neighbors or fought their friends. Fighting was so important they even killed their girl babies rather than see them grow up and marry an enemy and give birth to more enemies.

With a people who killed their own daughters, Esteban and the two captains passed a year in constant fear. They could do nothing else. They were surrounded by water, moving constantly from small island to small island. If the captives tried to escape and reach Pánuco by continuing along the coast, they knew they would soon become lost and drown in the marshes.

Dorantes decided that drowning was better than staying where he was. At noon one August day he escaped. Since the Karankawans said nothing more about him, Esteban and Castillo felt certain he had succeeded. In November, Esteban saw his chance and he too escaped. Castillo remained with the Indians.

8

Prickly Pears

"... and that day he crossed a great water and walked all he could with much fear. The next day he spoke with some Indians who took him with pleasure because they had already noticed that the Christians served well."

THESE Indians too were Karankawans, but kinder to Esteban than the band from whom he had escaped. To Dorantes, however, they had seemed equally dreadful. Soon after Esteban's arrival, he fled back toward the east. There he was captured by still another group of Karankawans.

Like the people of the coast, Esteban's new masters were always moving, always looking for food. During the winter they lived mostly on roots. But the Karankawans would eat anything from ant eggs to rats. They actually fought over

To gather the fleshy prickly pears, Indians walked many days across the dry thorny land. Juicy when ripe, the pears were sometimes dried in the sun and stored in baskets for use later.

more tasty animals, such as frogs, snakes, and lizards. Husbands grabbed food from their wives, mothers snatched it from their children, and the children stole it from the slave. They even fought for bones, which were pounded into a sort of flour. Often they were so hungry they ate animal droppings. To survive, Esteban imitated his new masters.

Still, he knew better times were coming. The Karankawans talked constantly of the happy season when they met their friends in certain thickets. Then, it seemed, they picked some kind of fruit. Their bellies grew fat. And even before that, things got better.

In April and May the rivers flooded, and fish moved upstream to lay their eggs. The Karankawans set their traps across streams and waited for the fish, bows in hand. Often there were so many fish they could catch them in their hands. They ate all they caught. But when the fish stopped coming, the people went hungry again. Apparently, the Karankawans had not discovered a way to dry or smoke fish to keep it from spoiling.

When the rivers returned to their normal banks and the ground was dry and hard enough for travel, the band started west toward the famous thickets.

It was about noon four or five days later when Esteban saw his first prickly pears. The pale green cactus pads looked almost silver. He rubbed his eyes. And yes, along the pads glowed bright red fruits—the fruits they had come to pick.

Shouting, the boys ran forward to pick the pears. They tumbled on the ground, stuffing the fruit into their mouths. Men and women ran to pick pears.

Esteban bit into a fruit and spat. He peeled off the rough skin and tried again. He ate pear after pear until his beard was sticky with juice.

Through the summer the band moved slowly north and westward gathering fruit. And from the great plains to the north and the hills to the west other tribes came. Friends greeted friends, and enemies forgot their differences. Together they celebrated the ripeness of the pears. Only when the pears became too ripe—and so too sour—did the tribes turn back toward their winter territories.

Encircling the swift pronghorns with fire, the Karankawans drove them into tight herds. Then they killed the pronghorns and other smaller animals trying to escape the fires.

The winter of 1531-32 was colder than the one before. But now Esteban had a buffalo robe to curl up in at night. He had gotten it by making such things as nets and bows, to trade with tribes from the plains. And soon he had Castillo to share his daily tasks of carrying wood and water. For that captain had finally escaped the cruel people of the coast and was taken by Esteban's new masters.

Best of all, the cold drove herds of pronghorns south to their usual range and into Karankawan territory. The Karankawans killed the antelope-like animals and many smaller

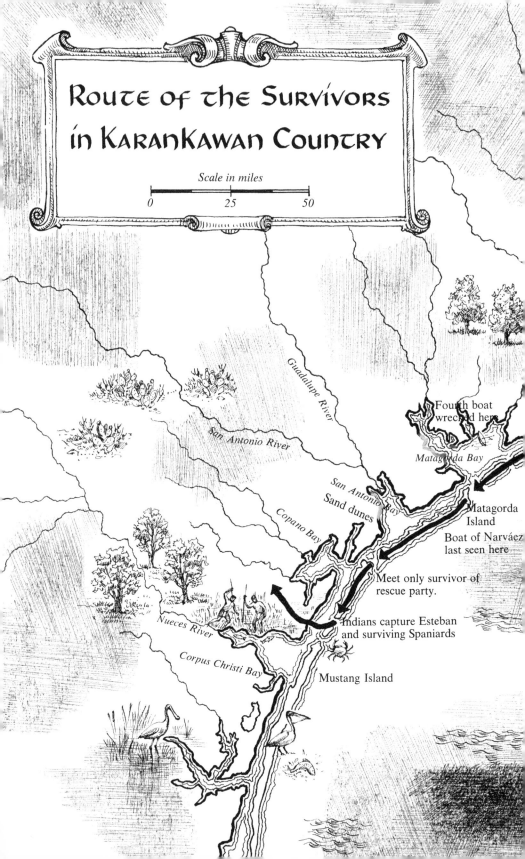

Route of the Survivors in Karankawan Country

Scale in miles

0   25   50

Guadalupe River

San Antonio River

Fourth boat wrecked here

Matagorda Bay

San Antonio Bay

Sand dunes

Copano Bay

Matagorda Island

Boat of Narváez last seen here

Meet only survivor of rescue party.

Indians capture Esteban and surviving Spaniards

Nueces River

Corpus Christi Bay

Mustang Island

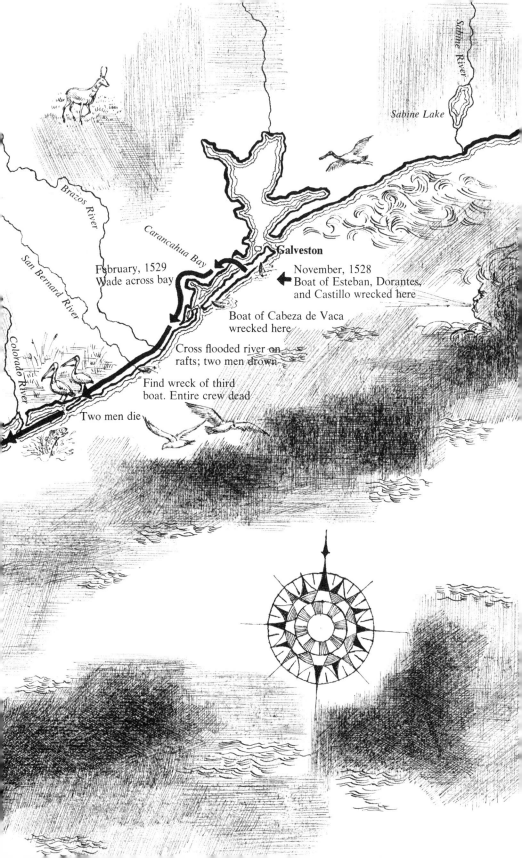

Sabine River

Sabine Lake

Brazos River

Carancahua Bay

San Bernard River

Galveston

February, 1529
Wade across bay

November, 1528
Boat of Esteban, Dorantes,
and Castillo wrecked here

Boat of Cabeza de Vaca
wrecked here

Colorado River

Cross flooded river on
rafts; two men drown

Find wreck of third
boat. Entire crew dead

Two men die

ones too. For days the smell of roasting meat drifted in the smoke of the campfires. In all his months in North America —in all his life—never had Esteban eaten so well and so much. The meat gave him new strength—and hope.

That summer when the prickly pears were once again ripe, Esteban met Andrés Dorantes among the cactus thickets. He refused to go with his former master—or so Dorantes later claimed. Perhaps Esteban was thinking of going north alone. If he found the Indians who hunted the pronghorns all the time, he could live a free man—free from hunger, free from fear. With Dorantes he would end his days a slave.

Before Dorantes and Castillo had made any definite plans, however, the two Indian bands separated. Castillo's and Esteban's masters followed a big river upstream to pick pecans, while Dorantes' masters continued farther east.

Late that fall Esteban saw Dorantes again. With him was another white man, Cabeza de Vaca. He had recovered from his illness and become a trader among the Indians of the woodlands. Friendly Indians had agreed to guide him down the coast toward Pánuco. On the way he had been captured by Dorantes' masters. Now he urged the other three to escape and continue west with him. This time Dorantes was the one who refused.

"We should wait out the winter with the Indians," he argued. "We will surely starve if we try to cross unknown territory in the cold."

"Or we may be killed," Castillo added. This they knew

While gathering prickly pears and nuts, Esteban met Indians from distant places, as well as the nearby Atakapas. This painting, made by a French artist many years later, shows a dancer with rattles and includes a black youth.

from the Indians had been the fate of the survivors from two other boats. Narváez's own boat appeared to have been lost at sea.

"We will meet again in the spring," Dorantes said. "By then the pears will be ripe. We'll find food as we go and we can give the Indians a good fight if they try to stop us."

The other Spaniards agreed to wait.

When the next prickly pear season came, however, the masters of Esteban and Castillo had quarreled with the masters of Dorantes and Cabeza. The four men were not able to meet as they had planned.

In September a year later they succeeded in escaping, but more by accident than plan. Shortly before the new moon, Esteban happened upon Dorantes' trail. With the help of an old Indian, Esteban and Castillo soon found the other two Spaniards. Before the moon was full, the territory of the Karankawans lay well behind them.

9

On the Inland Trail

"As we proceeded that day . . . we saw smoke. And going toward it, we reached the place after sundown. There we found an Indian who, when he saw us coming, did not wait, but ran away.

"We sent the Negro after him. And as the Indian saw him approach alone, he waited. The Negro told him that we were going in search of the people that make the smoke. He answered that the dwellings were nearby and that he would guide us, and we followed. He hurried ahead to tell of our coming."

THOUGH a strong runner, Esteban could not keep up with the guide. He was still some distance from the main camp when four Indians rushed out to greet him.

Esteban held his hands over his ears to show that he was deaf to their language. Then the Indians tried a Karankawan dialect that they used while trading during the prickly pear season. (Now they were returning north to their own territory.)

Esteban understood and went over to a small campfire. The air was already cool, and he missed the buffalo robe he had had to leave behind.

When the three Spaniards entered the camp, the women brought prickly pears. Everyone ate and smiled and ate some more. But when they were finished, several men came over to the strangers and spoke in harsh tones. Esteban jumped to his feet. Had he been mistaken about these people's friendly welcome? The women drew back a little with the children. All watched the black man.

"We have heard of your medicine," the Indians said. "Make us well." If Esteban did not know each word, he could not mistake the signs. The men were holding their heads and frowning with pain.

Suddenly Esteban remembered. Somehow, after all these years, these people had heard about the cures that Captain Castillo had made on the island. They wanted Castillo to cure them.

When Esteban told Castillo, the Spaniard nodded miserably.

"With God's help, I will try. But why have they given us food before the cures?"

Tramping across the bush-covered desert, Esteban and the three Spaniards sometimes saw a peccary rooting about for lizards. Perhaps they even ate the meat of this wild pig.

Esteban did not know. Before he could ask, the patients had settled themselves on the ground before Castillo. Around them sat their families.

Slowly Castillo traced the sign of the cross on each forehead. He blew gently on their heads, and he prayed. Again he made the sign of the cross over each patient. Nobody moved. Esteban could see Castillo's lips moving in prayer.

At last the patients rose. "It is as we heard," they said, smiling. Their headaches were gone.

Now the whole camp crowded about the "medicine man." The Indians touched his hands, his arms, his body, as though to get some of his medicine for themselves. The cured patients brought him chunks of dried deer meat and baskets heaped with pears.

Soon the camp rang with songs and the sound of dancing feet. With a maker of strong medicine among them, the Indians felt they could come to no harm. They rejoiced for three days and three nights, hardly stopping for sleep. Esteban was amazed at how long these people could celebrate without getting tired.

Esteban spoke quietly with the headman, trying to learn what he could about the hilly country that was the territory of these people. In his report, Cabeza de Vaca called them the Avavares.

"To the west," the headman told Esteban, "you will starve when the prickly pears are gone. You will freeze when the cold comes down from the mountains. You will die in the land where the sun goes down. Stay with us and live," the Avavare said.

When Esteban repeated this to the Spaniards, they decided to spend the winter with the Avavares. In the spring they would talk again of going westward.

As the winter came on, Esteban wondered if perhaps the headman had been describing his own territory. They found little to eat once the prickly pears were gone. For a time they picked mesquite beans, but after that they lived mostly on roots and bark.

The best food they gave to their children. But even so, the children were "so feeble and swollen they looked like toads," Dorantes said.

Fortunately Indians from other tribes came to Castillo

After pounding the bitter mesquite beans into a meal, the women mixed this with earth. Then they put the mixture into a small woven basket and added water, producing a sweet-tasting "bread."

during the winter. They brought food to exchange for his cures. Before long, Cabeza de Vaca began taking over the worst cases. Then Esteban and Dorantes too began to treat the sick. And as news of their cures spread, people came from far off just to let their children be touched by the "medicine men."

To be treated with such honor and respect was a new experience for Esteban. For all four it was a pleasant change after their years of slavery. Still they hoped to find better country. With luck they might yet reach Pánuco. The Spaniards talked continually of how they would get there. They did not want to return south to the trail along the coast. The risk of being captured again by the Karankawans was too great. They thought they might continue west, keeping more or less parallel to the coast, and then turn south, avoiding the Karankawans altogether.

In June, Cabeza and Esteban set off to explore up the river. They soon met people who were going west gathering persimmons and hackberries. Esteban went back for the two captains. Two days later the four men were on the trail westward.

10

The Children of the Sun

"From there they went on to other Indians two leagues forward, who gave them many things because of the cures, and who made many feasts and gave them very good food of cactuses and meat and went to hunt solely for the Christians; and there they became somewhat stronger. . . . The Indians made much of them and gave them all they had with very good will . . ."

ALL along the river the four "medicine men"—three Spaniards and one African—met small bands of friendly Indians gathering berries and hunting small game. Always they stopped and blessed the people before going on.

Esteban listened to their stories about plants that grew along the river, about small animals that watched them as they passed. The Indians talked to him about the customs of their country and the lives of their grandfathers. But nothing they said prepared him for the welcome he received late one afternoon. An entire village had come out on the trail to greet them. Shouting and screaming, they came. Two men led the others, tossing their long black hair from side to side and shaking their rattles.

Esteban took a step backward. There were so many people. And the rattles—they were made of gourds. Gourds meant planted fields. They meant people who farmed and lived in one place.

"Ask them about the gourds," Dorantes said impatiently.

Esteban tried the Avavare language. The Indians shook their heads. Then he tried all the other Indian languages he knew. It was no use. These people spoke a language he had not heard before.

The Indians listened carefully. Then the tallest man touched Esteban's cheek shyly. He rubbed the skin gently, and then harder. He looked at his fingers to see if the black had come off.

The other man tugged at Esteban's beard.

"Are you a man?" he asked.

Esteban understood the sign. "I come from across a great water," he said, also using signs. "I come from beyond the place where the sun rises."

In awe the two Indians drew back. "Then you must be the child of the sun." They put their arms across their eyes as

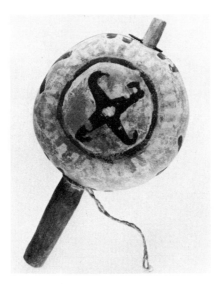

Many tribes used rattles in their ceremonial dances and in curing the sick. Some rattles were made by filling dry gourds with pebbles. Others were of buffalo hide or turtle shells.

though looking at the sun itself. The stones inside their gourds clicked softly.

Esteban smiled and reached for a gourd.

Its owner drew back angrily. Only shamans and other important men could carry rattles, and then only at special times.

The gourd was sacred. That was easy to understand. Esteban picked up a stick and traced a vine in the dust. He drew a gourd on the vine.

The taller Indian shook his head. He made the sign for water.

Esteban was excited. People must be raising gourds, and not too far away. When the rivers flooded, they washed over

Big Spring

July, 1535
Receive gourd rattles

Indians call Esteban
and Spaniards children
of the sun

Concho River

Indians welcome Esteban
and Spaniards as healers

EDWARDS PLATEAU

Pecos River

Rio Grande

Route of the
Survivors
InLand

Scale in miles

0   30   60

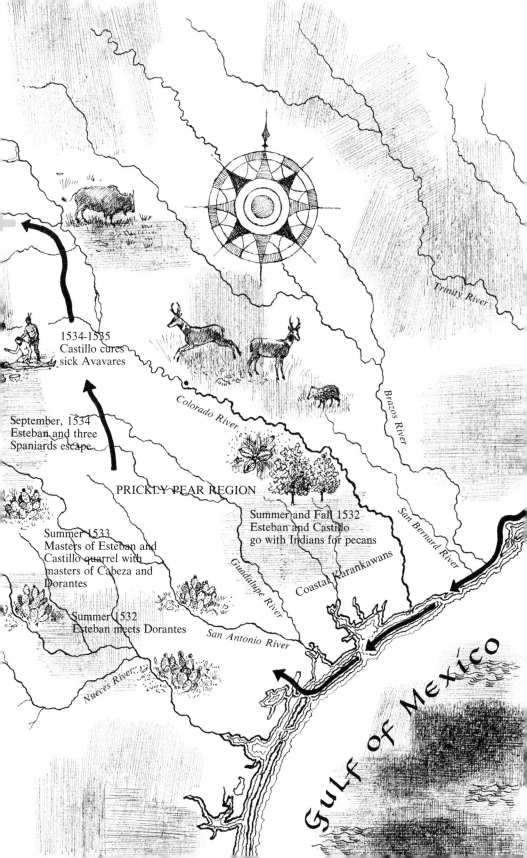

1534-1535
Castillo cures
sick Avavares

September, 1534
Esteban and three
Spaniards escape

PRICKLY PEAR REGION

Summer 1533
Masters of Esteban and
Castillo quarrel with
masters of Cabeza and
Dorantes

Summer and Fall 1532
Esteban and Castillo
go with Indians for pecans

Summer 1532
Esteban meets Dorantes

Colorado River

Trinity River

Brazos River

San Bernard River

Guadalupe River

Coastal Karankawans

San Antonio River

Nueces River

GULF OF MEXICO

Esteban surely tripped over an armadillo's burrow or saw anthills ripped apart by its strong, sharp paws.

the fields where the gourds were growing. The gourds were carried downstream to these people. That must be it.

But Esteban had no time for more questions. The villagers were crowding around him, trying to touch him. He felt himself being lifted up. The Indians rushed him along to a straw hut prepared in his honor. They brought food and water. All night long the people of the village danced and sang by their fires.

This time when the Spaniards and Esteban had cured the sick and were ready to leave, all the people of the village went with them. Ahead marched four Indians, each dressed like a medicine man in buffalo skin and sandals. One had rubbed soot over his face and chest. The other three had painted their faces with a white powder. All four carried gourd rattles, which they shook as they walked. They were going to prepare the next village for the coming of the "children of the sun."

When Esteban saw how they prepared the next village, he wished he had never spoken to these people. Almost immediately they began looting the village. They gathered up everything they could carry away. Though Esteban knew a few words of their language, he could not stop them.

"We told them you are the children of the sun, and you wish it," the tall Indian tried to reassure Esteban. "We told them to give all they have. If they hide anything, the sun will tell you."

Esteban shook his head.

"You have the power to save or destroy," the Indian said. "That is what we told them."

The looting did not seem to bother the villagers. If anything, they looked pleased. The looters had brought the wonderful medicine men.

"This custom is not bad," Dorantes commented. "Look, we shall have all the guides we need now. They have to guide us to the next village to make up for their losses!"

And this was just what happened. From then on, the people of one village guided the "medicine men" to the next village. They took their reward and returned home. And the people of the next village did the same.

Always four Indians, dressed as medicine men, went ahead to prepare the way.

11

The Other Side of the Mountain

"We travelled among so many different tribes and languages that nobody's memory can recall them all. And always they robbed each other, but those who lost and those who gained were equally content. . . . Those people set before us all the game they caught. They did not dare to touch the food, even if dying of hunger, unless we blessed it first. . . . The women brought many mats with which they built us houses . . ."

Bands of Indians began to travel with them rather than turning back. With hundreds of people, with women carrying babies on their backs, with children so young they could scarcely walk, Esteban and the three Spaniards continued on westward. The days were hot, and often the people stopped

70

and rested at noon. When the sun was lower in the sky, they went on.

Every day more people joined them. Later, Cabeza and Dorantes argued. Had 1,500 Indians gone with them or twice that number? However many there were, it was hard to walk with so many, and Esteban became impatient with their slow pace. Taking one or two guides with him, he often went on ahead.

One afternoon he noticed a great dark mass looming along the horizon.

"Is that a storm cloud?" he asked. They were still some distance from the village where they would camp that night.

The woman who was his guide that day smiled.

"Those are great hills," she said. "They sweep down to the roaring water." The woman made the sign for a big body of water.

Esteban frowned. "No, we do not want to go there."

"But we shall find other people there, many people for you to cure. Those people have fine things," the woman protested.

Esteban thought of the Karankawans and shook his head. He pointed to the trail leading west toward the mountains.

"There are no people that way," the guide replied. "It is better to go south now toward the great waters." She pointed out the southern trail. It was the most direct route to New Spain, or Mexico. But with all his skills in understanding signs, Esteban did not realize what the woman was saying.

The American artist George Catlin painted these Plains Indians creeping up on buffalo more than a hundred years ago. Then, as in Esteban's time, they shot only at close range.

The Spaniards shared Esteban's feelings. They did not want to take a chance on risking their lives among the Karankawans again. So they continued on west toward the mountains.

In the foothills of the mountains Dorantes was given a rattle of copper. When they looked at it closely, the Spaniards were sure their choice was correct. The rattle had a human face pounded out on its surface.

"I've seen such faces before," Cabeza said eagerly. "On treasures Cortés brought from Mexico."

When Esteban asked the Indian how he got it, the Indian gestured toward the west.

From this information, the Spaniards reasoned that the trail on the western side of the mountains must lead to Mexico. So with the Indians still objecting, they climbed the mountains. Taking a pass that appeared to be much traveled, they crossed the mountains and stood at last on the other side.

There was no great city in view. To the north lay hills of black lava. To the west stretched a vast white "sea." To the south they saw more mountains. Perhaps the trail along the eastern slope would have been better after all.

But a pleasant smoke filled the air and they camped that night in a large village. The villagers greeted them with beads and buffalo blankets. The women brought them piñon nuts pounded into soft sweet balls.

Esteban pulled his blanket close about him, enjoying the warmth. "Where did you get your shawl?" he asked the woman, who served him.

"From the west," she said. "Far to the west people live who make this cloth. They live in tall houses and don't move about."

"Do they grow the thread for this cloth?" Esteban asked. He saw that the three Spaniards were watching the woman's signs intently.

"No. The thread comes from the people on the coast. Far to the west." She held out another piñon ball.

Esteban chewed thoughtfully. That coast could not be the coast where the Karankawans lived. It must be the Pacific Ocean. They might reach Mexico, following that shore.

Esteban showed the Indians the copper rattle. The villagers nodded. They had seen such work before.

"The people of the tall houses work that metal," they said.

"That must mean . . ." Dorantes could not speak.

"The Seven Cities," Castillo finished softly.

"If only we had some gold, you could ask about that." Dorantes frowned. "Then we could be sure."

"We must go on at once," Cabeza said.

Esteban asked the villagers to guide them west.

"The cities you want are very far," they said. "There are no people on the way. There is nothing to eat, nothing to drink." The Indians acted out the horrors of the way west.

"Let us take you south," they begged.

This time the Spaniards and Esteban agreed. For as the morning haze lifted, they saw that the white "sea" shining before them was sand. They knew they could not cross a desert on their own.

For more than a month they struggled south along the foothills of the mountains. Every so often the Indians left the trail and entered the steep-walled canyons. They knew where each small spring was, and without them the "children of the sun" would have died of thirst.

As they came out onto the plain, Esteban asked each new band of Indians to guide them west, and always he was refused.

"Our enemies live to the west." There was no mistaking their signs. "We do not go there."

Gazing out at the endless white sands to the west, Esteban and the three Spaniards agreed to follow their guides southward.

But one day, after much talking, Esteban persuaded a woman to guide them. Women were respected as neutrals even in enemy territory. But of the Spaniards only Castillo volunteered to go on ahead with the black man.

"She took us to a river that flows between mountains," the captain remembered later. "There was a village. These were the first abodes that we saw that were like real houses." They had mud walls and thatched roofs.

But though the houses looked quite permanent, there were few people in the village—three or four old men and some women with tiny babies. Everyone else had gone north, it seemed, to hunt buffalo.

Few as they were, the villagers welcomed the strangers gladly with ripe melons. They were Jumanos, and they grew melons, beans, and squashes in their fields. Beyond the village a broad trail ran along the river. This looked promising.

"I'll go back and tell Dorantes and Cabeza," Castillo said. "You, Esteban, get some food together and meet us on the trail. Perhaps one of the women from this village will guide us. Do your best to persuade someone." Castillo and their guide rested and were gone.

Who can guess what Esteban thought that night as he crouched by the fire. A young Indian woman was cooking his supper in a way he had not seen before. She poured water into a gourd husk. Quickly and skillfully she dropped in two stones, hot from the fire. The stones were so hot that they made the water bubble.

Perhaps Esteban should go north and join the buffalo hunters. They would receive him well, he felt sure.

The woman added more hot stones to keep the water boiling. Then she poured in a flour of pounded beans. Round and round went her flat wooden paddle.

The Spaniards, Esteban thought, would never come after him. They wanted only to reach the Seven Cities or, anyway, Mexico City.

The woman picked out the stones and passed the gourd full of mush to Esteban. When he had eaten, he persuaded her to become their guide west. He had made his choice.

12

The Town of Hearts

"While travelling we used to go the whole day without food. At night we ate so little that the Indians were amazed. They never saw us tired because we were, in reality, so used to hardships that we did not notice them any more.

"We had great authority over them. In order to maintain it we spoke very little to them. It was the Negro who talked to them all the time. He asked about the trail we should follow, about the villages—in short, about everything we wished to know."

THE four—Esteban and the three Spaniards—went north along the river and then turned toward the sunset. The Jumano Indians had no fears, it seemed, about going westward. All along the trail they met other Jumanos, some going

On the plains beyond the Chiricahua mountains, Esteban and the Spaniards met people with nothing but dry desert grasses to offer them. For more than three weeks they walked, eating only such grasses and a handful of deer fat each day.

north for buffalo, others settling into their winter camps. Esteban soon began to understand their language very well.

The Jumanos led them along an easy trail, though mountains towered above them on every side. They walked west and then southwest into a wide valley. If they kept on walking, the guides told Esteban, they would reach the sea. It was not very far. This meant that the four had crossed the continent, and Spanish territory certainly lay somewhere to the south. However, the Jumanos could tell Esteban nothing of that land or of its white conquerors.

The people of the valley spoke a different language, and once again Esteban had to use signs to ask his questions. These people knew no more than the Jumanos of any other white men. They quickly understood that the four strangers were the "children of the sun," however. They gave them food and other presents. They touched the strangers and asked for their blessing.

Seeing this, the Jumanos left the four men and returned to their own territory. The "medicine men" went on south with the valley people as guides.

They came to large fields where squashes, corn, and beans were growing. Sometimes there were groups of flat-roofed houses clustered at the edge of a field. The houses belonged to the people whom the Spaniards called Pimas.

Along one river the four found three small towns where most of the people were ill. For several days they treated the sick. During this time the Pimas gave them many presents, including six hundred deer hearts, which had been dried and stored in clay pots. Because of this gift, Dorantes called the place the "pueblo de los corazones," or "town of hearts."

Of all the Indians they had met, the Spaniards admired most the women of this town. The Pimas wore long cotton shirts under deerskin jumpers which reached almost to the ground. On their feet they wore not straw or hide sandals as other Indians did, but soft deerskin moccasins. Esteban quickly threw away the buffalo hide sandals that the Jumanos had given him. A Pima woman made him a pair of moccasins decorated on top with beads and feathers.

"In the north the men cover their legs with deerskin," she told him. "They have fine clothes, too, and many fine stones like these." She touched the turquoise in her ear.

"What are these pink stones?" Esteban asked, pointing to the coral beads on his moccasins.

"Those come from the coast. But the people there are very poor. They don't even grow corn. They eat straw."

"Our land is dry like theirs," her father said. "But our fathers taught us how to water our fields. We dig ditches to bring water from the river. We use that water for our crops."

"Sometimes we pick corn three times in one year," the Pima girl said, slapping lumps of ground corn into flat cakes.

"And did your fathers make your fine houses, too?" Esteban asked. For certainly the Pima houses looked solid enough to

The hearts of bighorn sheep were certainly among the deer hearts presented to the "medicine men." During the winter the sheep moved into the lower valleys, where they were more easily hunted.

Some houses in which the Pimas lived, though often made of bear grass and brush, were very solid. Sun-baked mud around the base and on the roof kept out wind and rain and snow.

stand for years. Strong wooden beams held up their mud walls and roofs.

"Yes, our fathers and their fathers built our houses. They learned from the people of the north."

"What people do you mean?" Esteban ran his hand over the smooth mud roof of a house. "We have seen nothing so fine as your houses in all this land." The roof had been washed with lime, and the white came off on his hand.

"Far to the north, in the plains beyond the mountains, there are many people," the Pima said. "They make fine houses with many levels. Four, five, even ten. From their tall houses you can look to the four winds."

"And they decorate their houses with green stones," a Pima boy said.

"How do you know all these things?" Esteban asked.

"My father went there to trade," the boy said.

"There are many great towns in that country," another man added. "There are seven great towns, maybe more. Many families make their houses in those towns."

It seemed the old legends were true. The Seven Cities existed after all, and not so far away.

"You trade with these people?" Esteban tried to control his eagerness.

"Yes," said the Pimas. "They give us cotton and turquoise. We give them feathers and deerhides. Sometimes we give them beans and squashes."

"Where do you get the feathers?" Esteban tied a soft white feather to his gourd rattle and then added a bright red one.

"From the south."

"From the south where the white men are?"

The Pimas looked puzzled. "From the south," they repeated. They knew nothing of any other white men.

But when Esteban and the Spaniards started south, many men and women offered to come as guides. The little children ran along with them for some distance. They gave Esteban and each of the Spaniards four corn kernels to keep them safe till they found their white brothers.

13

A Buckle, a Horseshoe Nail, and Chains

"After leaving this town, they went 30 leagues to a river . . .
where it rained fifteen days and they had to stop. . . . There
Castillo saw an Indian with a piece of sword belt and a
horseshoe nail hung from his neck like a jewel."

ESTEBAN had seen necklaces of beans and nuts, of animal
teeth, shells, and beads. Sometimes he wore one himself. But
he had never seen a necklace like this.

"Ask him where he got it," Castillo said, excitedly. "That's
a Spanish buckle. I know it."

Esteban pointed to the necklace.

With a worried look, the Indian gestured toward the sky.

"It came from the sky?" Esteban repeated.

"Other men came with white skins," the Indian told Esteban. "They had beards. They came from the sky to the river."

The Indian's friends acted out what had happened. They galloped like horses, then pulled imaginary swords. The first man fell to the ground, making terrible cries.

"Where did the bearded men go?" Esteban asked.

"To the sea." The Indians pointed to the west. "They went into the sunset riding on top of the water."

Esteban frowned. Other white men had raided this country. It was easy to see where they had been. Everywhere houses were burned and fields ruined. Most of the people were in hiding.

Still the three Spaniards felt joyful. Their countrymen must be nearby. Soon they would be with civilized people. Their hardships would be over.

Cabeza de Vaca called Esteban to one side. "Our Pimas had better go home," he said. "Tell them to go and plant their fields. We can find the trail ourselves. They really must go home."

Esteban agreed. But the Pimas refused to obey. They did not want to return home until they met other people who could receive the "medicine men" properly.

"Then let them send out messengers in our names," Cabeza suggested. "Let them tell the people of this country that the 'children of the sun' will not allow the bad white men to carry them into slavery. We shall make them stop. They have my word."

Watching a bold raccoon-like coati (right) or a ring-tailed caco-mistle balancing on a pine branch at sunset, Esteban may have for-gotten his worries about the Indians taken as slaves.

The Pima messengers were unable to deliver their message. They returned with frightening news. They had seen thousands of Indians chained together, marching down the coast.

Even then, the Pimas wanted to keep on with the four strangers. Nothing Esteban said could shake their determination.

A few days later, Esteban saw stakes that had been used to tie horses. From the horse droppings he knew that the animals had been there only a few days ago.

"If we go quickly, we can catch up with them," Cabeza said.

"But they have horses," Castillo protested.

"I am too tired for a forced march like that," Dorantes grumbled. "You and Esteban go. Castillo and I will stay here

Tucson •

Chiricahua Peak

Indians give corn,
beans, and cotton

Gulf

of

Town of Hearts

Sonora River

January, 1536
Delayed by floods

Meet Indian wearing
buckle and horseshoe nail

Yaqui R.

Obregon •

CALIFORNIA

PACIFIC OCEAN

Fuerte River

Gila Cliff Dwellings

October, 1535
Plains Indians give
piñon nuts

White Sands

Dorantes is given
copper rattle

Esteban and Spaniards
receive cornmeal

Las Cruces

November, 1535
Buffalo people
give beans, squashes,
and gourds

Meet desert people who
eat dried herbs all winter

El Paso

Carlsbad Caverns

Pecos

Pecos River

Rio Grande

CONTINENTAL DIVIDE

Chihuahua

SIERRA MADRE

1536
New Spain

Scale in miles

0   50   100

Meet Melchior Díaz

Culiacán

Durango

To Mexico City

and round up the people who are still in hiding."

So Cabeza and Esteban went ahead with eleven or twelve Pimas. A day later they came upon four Spanish horsemen camped by a fire. Their captain agreed to guide them south toward Culiacán. In that town Melchior Díaz, who was their commander and an official of the Spanish government, made his headquarters.

Esteban and Cabeza went back for the others, and all proceeded to Culiacán, where they found Díaz. He knew about the Narváez expedition but, like everyone else, he had assumed that all had died. He greeted the four survivors with respect. But when he counted the Indians they had brought, he became truly enthusiastic.

"You must have 1,000 slaves here," he said. "Or more."

"These men and women are not slaves," Cabeza said quickly. "They are friends. They must be allowed to return to their homes and plant their fields. If we Christians are to settle in this land, we will need food and water. We will need the help of these people and of all the people like them."

Esteban watched Díaz's face. It told him nothing.

"If you will guarantee peace and freedom to the Pimas, I shall see that their help is given," Cabeza said.

At last, Díaz agreed. "I will do so," he said, "until His Majesty or the Viceroy instructs me differently." (The Viceroy was the ruler of New Spain, or Mexico.)

From hand to hand went Cabeza's medicine gourd. It gave authority to the other white man's words. Then the Pimas

Esteban followed his guides past towering saguaro cactuses like these.
The women used the fruit as they did the prickly pears.

asked for one last blessing from the "medicine men." Most
of them went home, though some families decided to settle
near Culiacán. Still others wanted to continue on south with
their "medicine men."

Two months later, escorted by these Pimas and by Spanish
soldiers from Culiacán, the four survivors of the Narváez
expedition rode into Mexico City.

14

In the Service of the Viceroy

"Three Spaniards named Cabeza de Vaca, Dorantes, and Castillo Maldonado, and a Negro, who had been lost on the expedition which Pánfilo de Narváez led into Florida, reached Mexico. They came out through Culiacán, having crossed the country from sea to sea. . . . They gave the good Don Antonio de Mendoza a long account of some powerful villages, four and five stories high. They had heard a great deal about these villages in the countries which they had crossed."

THE soldier who wrote this, one Pedro Castañeda, was in Mexico City when the four survivors arrived. He met and talked with Esteban. About thirty years later he wrote a brief account of the black man's part in the discovery of

North America. Unfortunately, he wrote nothing of Esteban's months in Mexico City. However, Esteban's first job was probably helping with the report to the Viceroy, Don Antonio de Mendoza. The Viceroy wanted to hear all about the land they had crossed and the people they had seen. Future explorers would be glad to have such information.

Cabeza de Vaca reported to the Viceroy in person. The others did not have that honor, because they were not of noble birth. But all three Spaniards worked together on the written report. And Esteban, as Dorantes' slave, was called in often. He remembered the customs of each people. He knew the animals they had hunted and the plants they had become acquainted with. Esteban also corrected their maps of the "firm land" they crossed. Since he had discussed the good and bad points of each trail with the Indians, he added many details overlooked by the Spaniards who had followed him.

When the Viceroy had met with Cabeza several times and had read the full report, he realized the importance of their discoveries. Most of all he was excited by what they had heard about the seven tall cities of the north. Recently, Francisco Pizarro had found enormous wealth in Peru. Now, Mendoza might gain far greater riches from the north.

Viceroy Mendoza lost no time in applying for the King's commission to explore and settle that unknown territory. Without this, of course, he had no legal authority to do so. To make sure of the King's approval he sent along the joint report and the maps. These were lost at sea. (Luckily, the historian Oviedo had already read the report and included large parts of it in his history of the Indies. Cabeza's own report was published later.)

Mendoza did not wait for the King's reply. He began preparing for the expedition to the north. First he tried to get Captain Dorantes to lead it, but that plan did not work out. Like Castillo, Dorantes soon married and settled down near Mexico City. Their exploring days were over.

Cabeza de Vaca returned to Spain to apply for Narváez's old commission to explore the Florida territory. Since the King had already granted this to Hernando de Soto, Cabeza accepted appointment as governor in one of the Spanish provinces in South America.

Of the four survivors, Esteban alone was available.

But could the Viceroy trust so important an expedition to a slave, to a black? Mendoza feared not. Earlier that year black slaves had tried to lead Indian slaves against their Spanish masters in the mines of Mexico. True, the plot had been discovered, and the uprising put down. Twenty-four slaves had been hanged as a warning to other ambitious black men.

Besides, Esteban was no ordinary slave. To the Indians he was a god. He spoke at least six Indian languages. He could move freely and safely among many different tribes. He might even lead the people of the Seven Cities against the Spaniards.

Yet for the very reasons that Mendoza feared Esteban, he needed him. Esteban knew 3,000 miles of a continent

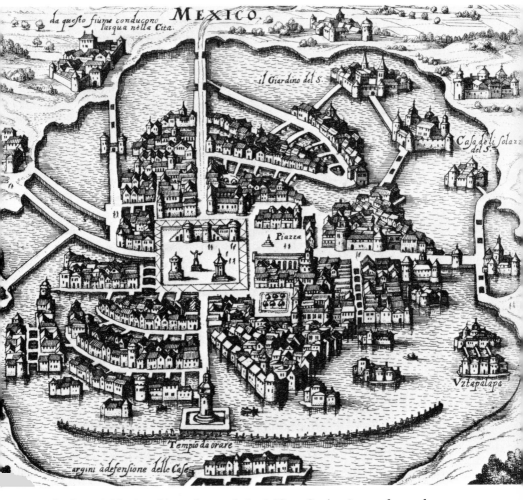

A plan of Mexico City, the capital of New Spain, from about the period when Esteban was there.

known only to the three white men who would not, or could not, lead the expedition. Mendoza had to have Esteban.

Andrés Dorantes refused to sell his slave. "He would not give him up," one witness reported, "for 500 pesos in a plate of silver, which the Viceroy sent as payment by a third person." In the end, Dorantes said that Esteban might "serve the Viceroy in the name of His Majesty, because of the good which might come to the souls of the natives in these provinces to the interests of the royal estate."

Of course, Mendoza could not let a slave—even a freed slave, an African—command an expedition. He appointed his friend, Francisco Vásquez de Coronado, to that post. Esteban was to serve as Coronado's advance scout. His job was to prepare the way for the Spanish army. Keeping the needs of both men and horses in mind, he was to lay out the best trails he could. He would locate watering holes and good supplies of food. He would study the defenses of the Seven Cities. If possible, he would try to persuade the people of the Seven Cities to surrender peacefully.

Such scouting activity in non-Spanish territory was no more legal than a full-scale expedition. Fortunately Friar Marcos, a priest who had been with Pizarro in Peru, offered to go along. And Mendoza did have the authority to send out small missionary parties to convert the Indians to Christianity.

The King wanted souls to be saved, the priest pointed out. This he would do, even if they found no golden cities. Besides, he was a good map-maker, and maps might be useful some day.

Pleased with this plan, Mendoza gave the priest orders for a missionary journey. He was careful to send a copy to the King.

A friar baptizes Indians in the background, as Spanish conquistadors count the treasures from the conquered peoples.

As well as saving souls, the priest was to make legal claim to the land in the King's name. If they did find the Seven Cities, the King would be delighted. He would have his usual share of the treasure and, with no cost to himself, the land would be his. He would surely excuse the Viceroy's failure to follow the letter of the law.

In the spring of 1539, everything was ready. Coronado and his soldiers escorted Esteban, Friar Marcos, and another priest as far as Culiacán. With them were a few Indian interpreters given them by Mendoza. Esteban also had two greyhounds, the parting gift, perhaps, of his master.

At Culiacán, they were joined by a great many Pima Indians, eager to go north with them. And on March 7, the missionary party started toward the Seven Cities, escorted now only by the Pimas.

15

On the Road to the Seven Cities

"The Negro did not get on well with the friars. He took the
women that were given him. He collected turquoises and
got together a stock of everything. Besides, the Indians in
those places they went through got along with the Negro
better, because they had seen him before. . . . These had followed him from all the settlements they had passed. They
believed that under his protection they could cross the
whole world without any danger."

Once on the trail, Esteban soon found that the priests were
in poor physical shape for the long march north. Friar Marcos
was no longer young and the other man became ill. Without
Esteban and the Pimas, the Spaniards would starve. Still, the
priests grumbled about everything Esteban did. He let the
Indian women carry the food and water. That was wrong,

97

the priests said. The women set up shelters for the night. That was wrong too. Esteban tried to explain that this was the custom of that country, but the Spaniards were too shocked to listen.

His heathen clothing bothered them too. For by this time Esteban had given away the hot European clothes he had worn in Mexico City. He wore only a loin cloth, though to please his Pima friends he wound a bracelet of parrot feathers around one wrist and tied a string of copper bells around each ankle. That was the style of their shamans.

The priests shook their heads. This barbaric person was their guide. Their lives depended on him. Yet even the prancing steps of his two little greyhounds mocked the Spaniards as they struggled along the trail.

But Esteban had little time to worry about them. From the countryside all around Indians came to greet the friend who had spared them from slavery. They brought food and many other presents. Esteban had to divide the presents fairly among the Pimas with him. And of course he had to cure the sick. Without the other three "medicine men," the treatment took just that much longer. The priests looked on in horror.

"This is the work of the devil," the sick priest said. "I am returning to Culiacán."

Alone then with Esteban and the Pimas, Friar Marcos split up the party. He sent some Indians west to explore the coast. Esteban and a few Indians he sent north to learn more about the Seven Cities.

Over a stove like this, Pima women prepared corn cakes or perhaps a rabbit stew for Esteban. Since coyotes and other animals roamed through the open kitchen, food was stored on the roof.

"I agreed with him," Friar Marcos told Mendoza later, "that if he learned of any people and rich country . . . he should go no farther but should return in person, or send me certain Indians with this token: that if it were but a mean thing he send me a white cross one hand long; if it was any great matter a cross two hands long; and if it were a country greater and better than Mexico he send me a great cross."

After dinner on March 23, 1539, Esteban left Friar Marcos. No white man ever saw him again, and so none wrote of his adventures going north toward the Seven Cities.

Four days later, the first messengers reached the priest.

Esteban's Route to Hawikuh

Scale in miles

0   50   100

HAWIKUH

Zuni

Phoenix

Gila River

Organ Pipe Cactus

Tucson

Chiricahua Peak

El Paso

Rio Grande

GULF OF CALIFORNIA

Town of Hearts

Sonora River

Son of Pima chief delivers news of Esteban

Four Indians make drawings of seven cities for Marcos

Marcos receives second great cross from Esteban

March 23, 1539 Esteban and his Pimas are sent on ahead

Second Indian group goes west toward coast

Yaqui R.

Fuerte River

They carried a very large cross. In the Seven Cities beyond the mountains, they said, the people were rich beyond belief. They wore clothes of fine cotton and placed green stones in their nostrils and ear lobes. They ate from gold dishes and scraped away their sweat with little plates of gold. The messengers added more details of this sort. But since the priest had often heard almost the same stories from Esteban himself, there seemed no reason to hurry. He needed to rest a few days more before going on.

Esteban did not wait for the priest to catch up. By the time Friar Marcos did start off, Esteban must have been north of the Sonora Valley. And as he went still farther north, the climate was cooler and walking easier. Each day he must have gained many miles on the priest.

To explain the black man's failure to wait for Friar Marcos as he had agreed, the soldier Casteñeda later suggested that Esteban wanted "all the reputation and honor himself. If he alone should discover those settlements with such famous high houses, he would be considered bold and courageous. So he proceeded with the people who had followed him and crossed the wilderness which lies between the country he passed through and the Seven Cities."

Far behind him, Friar Marcos tramped along in the heat. He rested in the huts Esteban's Indians had made and ate the food they left for him. At each such camp he found large crosses and other messages urging him to hurry.

One day some Indians drew a picture of one city in the

Like these pueblo women, those Esteban met wore cloaks of cotton and shoes of tanned deerskin reaching to the knees. The unmarried girls still wear their hair about their ears like little wheels.

sand. They showed the priest how the northern people built their tall houses, stone upon stone, and cemented the stones together with mud on the inside. Their method of building seemed far more complicated than anything the priest had seen among the Pimas. And somehow the drawing made the

Seven Cities seem more real. The old priest forced himself to cover more ground each day.

Still, he had to stop to take possession of the land in the King's name. And the result, according to Castañeda's report was that "Esteban was so far ahead of the priest that when this man reached Red Houses, a town on the edge of the wilderness, Esteban was already at the Seven Cities, which is 80 leagues beyond [or about 250 miles]."

Friar Marcos first knew this late one afternoon. The son of a Pima chief came running toward the priest. He came from Esteban, but he was too winded to speak. Toward sunset he was joined by two other Pimas. At last Friar Marcos was able to piece together their story. It was so frightening he decided to follow Esteban no farther. The next morning he headed back for Culiacán.

Coronado met him near that town and was much impressed with the priest's news. According to one witness, Friar Marcos "told such great things about what the Negro Esteban had discovered and what they had heard about the south sea and islands and other riches, that without stopping for anything Coronado set off at once for the City of Mexico, taking Friar Marcos with him, to tell the Viceroy about it."

Early the next spring Coronado started north on Esteban's trail.

16

The End of the Trail

"At one day's march from the city, Esteban sent his gourd with his messengers, as was his habit, to announce his arrival . . . .This gourd has a string of bells upon it and two feathers, one white and another red. . . . He told his messengers to tell the chief that he was coming to make peace and to cure the sick. . . .

"The messengers gave the chief the gourd. That man took it, and seeing the string of bells, became angry and threw it to the ground. He told the messengers to go away. 'I know these strangers,' he said. 'Tell them not to enter the city. Otherwise I will kill them all.'

"The messengers went back and told Esteban how they had been received. He said that it was nothing. Those who showed displeasure at his coming always received him better than the others.

"He continued on his way and arrived at the city. As he was about to enter, he found his way blocked. The Indians led him to a great house which was outside the city, and immediately took everything he carried: his objects for trading, the turquoises and many other presents he had received during his journey.

"He spent the night in that house without anyone giving him anything to drink or eat. They gave nothing to the people with him either. The next morning . . . Esteban went out of the house and some of the chiefs with him. Suddenly there came many people from the city. When he saw them, he began to run away and we with him. Immediately they shot at us . . .

"And on the terraces we saw many men and women watching, and after this we could not see Esteban any more. We believe they have shot him to death with arrows as they did the rest who went with him, so that only we escaped."

THIS was the Pimas' story as Friar Marcos reported it to the Viceroy. Mendoza was delighted with it. The slaying of Esteban gave him all the excuse he needed to send off an expedition without royal permission. A people called the Zunis had killed Esteban. The Spaniards would avenge his death. And in July, 1539, Coronado and his soldiers stormed and captured the Zunis' pueblo. It was a town the Zunis called Hawikuh.

From the defeated Zunis, Coronado heard a somewhat different account of what had happened to his scout. He repeated this in a letter to the viceroy later that summer:

The death of the Negro is perfectly certain, because many of the things he wore have been found. The Indians say that they killed him here, because the Indians of another pueblo said he was a bad man. They said he was not like the Christians, because the Christians never kill women, and the Negro killed them. . . .

Therefore they decided to kill him. But they did not do it in the way that was reported. They did not kill any of the others who came with him.

To the Spaniards, however, these facts were of little real interest. The important thing was that Hawikuh and the five or six other Zuni pueblos were not the Seven Cities of the old legends. For all their strong houses and beautiful clothes, the Zunis had no gold. For treasures like those of Mexico and Peru, the Spaniards would have to look elsewhere. With new guides, Coronado and his men went on to explore the country to the north and east.

But the soldier, Pedro Castañeda, was stationed in Hawikuh. And because he had known Esteban, he tried to find out what had happened. He learned that the Zunis had suspected Esteban of being a spy. "It seemed to them unreasonable to say that the people were white in the country from which he came and that he was sent by them, he being black."

The Zuni scouts had traveled south for three days. Since they found no white men, they concluded the black man was lying.

From the roofs of Hawikuh, the Zuni people watched Esteban. Like this one, the ancient pueblo, as described by a Spanish soldier, had walls of dirt and mud, and doors like hatchways of ships.

Then there was the medicine gourd. It looked suspiciously like the gourds used by the Plains Indians, and the red feather in itself was a sign of war. The Zunis were often at war with the people of the plains. Even in times of peace they did not trust them. When the Plains Indians came to trade, the Zunis made them leave their weapons outside the pueblo. Usually they asked their guests to sleep in the great house outside the pueblo too.

Of course, the scouts did not see war parties in that region. Yet if Esteban were not a spy, he was perhaps something much more dangerous. His followers said he was the child of the sun. He could drive out evil spirits with his medicine. If the Zunis gave him fine presents, the Pimas told them, they would see his medicine for themselves.

If the black man was truly a sorcerer, the verdict was clear. He must be killed. But the Zunis hesitated. They had no evidence.

Then Esteban himself settled the matter for them. By trying to run off, he proved his guilt to the Zunis. They shot him on the spot. They took a few Pimas as hostages, in case the black man had spoken the truth. They let all the others return home.

The Zunis then sent the dead man's bones out as a warning to all the tribes of that region: Death will come to any who attack the Zunis.

The message reached the people of the pueblos south and east along the Rio Grande. It traveled west all the way to the coast. Of course it did not reach Coronado. He marched north anyway. And after him came Spanish missionaries, miners, cattlemen, settlers. Eventually the old Zuni territory became part of the United States.

Still, the people of the pueblos told the story of Esteban. At special ceremonies, dancers wearing black masks acted it out. Fathers carved dolls in his image so that their children would learn and remember the black man's story, for his coming had changed their lives forever.

Here is one version that some Zunis sang to a white anthropologist less than one hundred years ago. (By Mexican, the Zunis mean any person who speaks Spanish.)

One day a long time ago
When roofs lay over the walls,
When the ladder rungs were unbroken,
The Indians came,
The Indians of Sonora.

The black Mexican brought them.
With long bows and cane arrows,
With war feathers,
Like no friends they came
From their land of everlasting summer.

So our bad-tempered grandfathers,
So quick to anger,
Rushed into the village,
Rushed out from the village,
Skipping,
Shouting,
Tossing war clubs,
Shooting sling stones and arrows.

And the Indians of Sonora howled,
They too shooting their arrows,
Harming our grandfathers.

Then where the stone stands
Down by the brook,
The black Mexican was killed.
Our grandfathers killed him,
A large man with chili lips.

Used to frighten children into good behavior, this doll carved by a pueblo Indian is supposed to represent Esteban. A long, bright red tongue hangs from the lower lip, and the eyes are yellow slits. The ogre wears a fur cape whose tail trails down the back and is just visible between the yellow leggings.

The Indians of Sonora ran.
They ran back to their country.
Our grandfathers chased them.

Then the Mexicans came
With their coats of iron,
With their thundersticks.
In fear-making bands they came.
They seized the life trails of our grandfathers.

EPILOGUE

The Verdict

Everyone knows that when two people tell a story about the same happening the two stories differ a little. Each time those two stories are repeated they differ still more. History is made of such tellings and retellings. And often it is hard to find out what really happened. That is especially true about Esteban.

We can be fairly sure that he was the prisoner of the Zunis. The Pimas and the Zunis and the Spaniards all agreed about that.

The Zuni elders met in their ceremonial chamber to discuss his case. That was their custom.

Was the black man a spy? That was the most urgent question. The scouts found no white people with weapons. Perhaps the black man was boasting about all his brothers, in

Inside their ceremonial chamber, the Zuni elders met to discuss Esteban's fate. This photograph from the 1880's is one of the few ever permitted inside such a chamber. The five men are treating a boy. Note their rattles.

order to scare his captors. If so, the Zunis would look foolish if they took him seriously.

Was he a sorcerer? In spite of the Pimas' claims, he had not worked his medicine among the Zunis.

The Zunis could not kill a man without a good reason, so they just threw him out. At least this is the version that is repeated by a famous historian of the Southwest.

One night, or so the story goes, the elders visited Esteban.

They dropped a ladder down from the roof into his room. They called to him, and Esteban climbed up. Before he could say anything, one of the elders gave him a powerful kick. This carried him through the air back toward the south and the land from which he came.

But if the Zunis did not kill Esteban, what became of him then? There is no reliable answer.

The Pimas would probably have hidden Esteban from the Zunis if they could. They also wanted to hide him from the Spaniards. To do this, they sent the three messengers to scare away Friar Marcos with the story of the massacre. To their delight, the priest rushed away as planned, which gave Esteban time to travel more slowly back to the safety of the Sonora Valley. If the Zunis had wounded him, it would have been important to have this extra time.

There is one clue to the rest of Esteban's story. This is a scrap of a document that was found some years ago among government records in Mexico. Here is what it says:

> Esteban arrived at the Rio Mayo, was struck by the beauty and handsomeness of the Mayos [who were close cousins of the Pimas], hid himself there and stayed. Later he married four or five women according to the custom of the land, had offspring, and in the year 1622 his son Aboray was living there, a tall withered mulatto with an ugly face, a captain or chief of a section of Tesia village...

The scrap bears the signature of a person named Ruíz. It

has no date and the rest of the document is missing.

Perhaps one day some one will prove that this Esteban was the very man the Zunis had held prisoner outside their pueblo. And then we will know that Esteban escaped and died a free man not far from the Pacific coast.

Until then we know only that the Zunis' prisoner was Esteban el Negro, born in Africa. And this Esteban was the man whose long walk across North America, west to the Pacific and north to the Zunis, prepared the way for Coronado and De Soto. Their discoveries, in turn, prepared the way for you and me.

A NOTE ON THE SOURCES

THE HISTORY of Esteban's life is based mainly on three reports, written during his lifetime or shortly after his death. These are:

The Journey of Álvar Núñez Cabeza de Vaca and His Companions from Florida to the Pacific 1528-1536. Translated from his own narrative by Fanny Bandelier. Together with the report of Father Marcos de Nizza and a letter from the Viceroy Mendoza. Edited with an Introduction by Adolph F. Bandelier. New York: 1905.

Gonzalo Fernández de Oviedo y Valdéz, *Historia general y natural de las Indias, islas y tierra-firma del mar océano.* Paraguay: 1945. Tomo X, libro 16, partito ii, capitulo i-vii, page 195 ff.

Pedro de Castañeda de Najera, "Narrative written for Viceroy Mendoza," in *The Journey of Coronado, 1540-42, From the City of Mexico to the Grand Cañon of the Colorado and the Buffalo Plains of Texas, Kansas, and Nebraska, as told by himself and his followers.* Translated and edited by George Parker Winship. New York: 1904.

The quotations that introduce chapters 1, 2, 4, 5, 6, 9, 10, 11, 12 are taken from Cabeza's narrative, as are the quotations within those chapters, except for chapter 9 where the quotation is from

Oviedo's history. All the quotations in chapters 3, 7, 8, and 13 are also from Oviedo. The quotations in chapters 14 and 15 are from Castañeda except for the excerpt from Friar Marcos' report, which may be found appended to Cabeza's narrative. A longer excerpt from this report introduces chapter 16. The quotation from the Coronado letter is from Frederick Webb Hodge, *History of Hawikuh, New Mexico,* One of the So-Called Cities of Cibola. Los Angeles: 1937.

The Zuni legend is adapted from F. Hamilton Cushing, "Zuni Breadstuff," in *Indian Notes and Monographs.* New York: 1920.

For the routing of Esteban's trail across the continent I have relied almost entirely on the three following works:

Cleve Hallenbeck, *Álvar Núñez Cabeza de Vaca. The Journey and Route of the First European to Cross the Continent of North America 1534-1536.* Glendale, California: 1940.

————, *The Journey of Fray Marcos de Niza.* Dallas: 1949.

Carl Sauer, "The Road to Cibola," in *Ibero-Americana: 3.* Berkeley, California: 1932.

SUGGESTIONS FOR FURTHER READING

Baker, Betty. *Walk the World's Rim.* Harper, 1965.

Baker, Nina B. *Juan Ponce de León.* Knopf, 1957.

Berger, Josef; Wroth, Lawrence C.; and the editors of *Horizon* Magazine. *Discoverers of the New World.* (American Heritage) Harper, 1960.

Bleeker, Sonia. *The Pueblo Indians.* Morrow, 1955.

_____. *The Seminole Indians.* Morrow, 1954.

Buehr, Walter. *The Spanish Conquistadores in North America.* Putnam, 1962.

Campbell, Camilla. *Coronado and His Captains.* Follett, 1958.

Dalgliesh, Alice. *America Begins: The Story of the Finding of the New World.* Scribner, 1958.

Day, A. Grove. *Coronado and the Discovery of the Southwest.* Meredith, 1967.

Glubok, Shirley. *The Art of the North American Indian.* Harper, 1964.

Jensen, Paul. *National Parks: A Guide to the National Parks and Monuments of the United States.* Golden Press, 1964.

Knoop, Faith Y. *Francisco Coronado.* Garrard, 1967.

La Farge, Oliver. *The American Indian.* Golden Press, 1963.

Marcus, Rebecca. *The First Book of the Cliff Dwellers.* Watts, 1968.

Mirsky, Jeannette. *The Gentle Conquistadors.* Pantheon, 1969.

Montgomery, Elizabeth Rider. *Hernando de Soto.* Garrard, 1964.

Scheele, William E. *The Earliest Americans*. World, 1963.

_____. *The Mount Builders*. World, 1960.

Sutton, Ann, and Sutton, Myron. *Guarding the Treasured Lands: The Story of the National Park Service*. Lippincott, 1965.

Wojciechowska, Maia. *Odyssey of Courage*. Atheneum, 1965.

INDEX

Page numbers in boldface refer to illustration captions or maps

About the Author

ELIZABETH SHEPHERD is a graduate of Bryn Mawr College, and a former teacher in the elementary grades. She has been a writer and editor for a children's encyclopedia, and is the author of the juvenile titles, IN A PYGMY CAMP and JELLYFISHES.

An enthusiastic hiker and amateur naturalist, she lives in New York City with her husband, son, and daughter. Her interest in Esteban stems from a study of American Indians of the southwest during which she came across mention of a black man in America in preconquest times. "To me," she says, "the saga of an untrained, unequipped slave surviving eight years in the wilderness, crossing a continent, and commanding the devotion of a whole people is far more heroic than the exploits of a computerized spaceman."

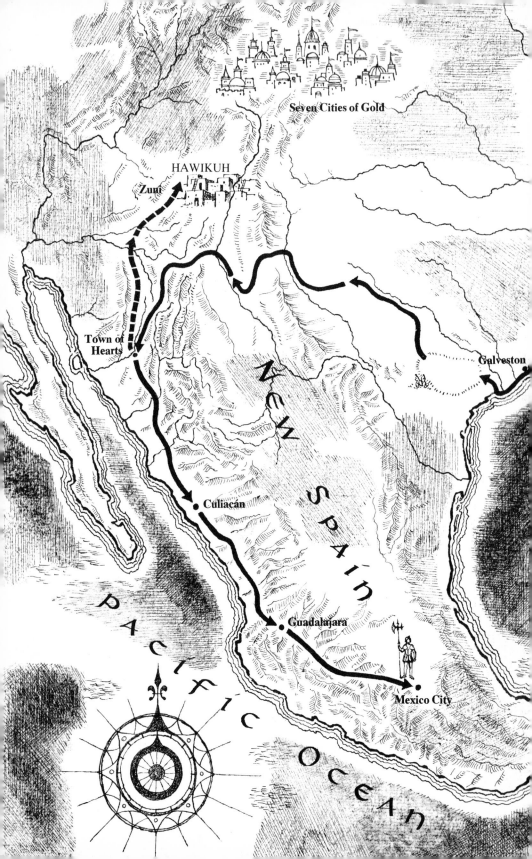